THE DAILY CHRISTIAN
PRAYER

IANN SCHONKEN

FREE GIFT FOR MY READERS

Thank you for exploring my book today. I have a special gift waiting for you online!

Use your smartphone's QRcode reader on the QRcode below, or go directly to the website for access to a free weekly newsletter and free ebooks to download for your reading pleasure.

—Iann

Website: www.thedailychristian.org/p/free-ebooks

CONTENTS

WHY THIS BOOK
EXISTS

FIRST OF ALL, thank you for picking up this book and allowing me to reach out to you in the busyness of your life. I always endeavor to encourage readers to reach up toward a loving God and to experience the positive effects of His benevolent Presence. I believe that being a follower of Jesus Christ is a daily walk rather than an occasional event.

The Daily Christian series of books is presented as a devotional tool that helps modern seekers and believers learn more about God in a simple, non-exhaustive manner amid their challenging lives. The series covers twelve topics where all can expect to see their lives change for the better as we follow the instructions presented in the Bible.

Each book will have an introductory chapter followed by twenty-one days of relatively short readings to progressively illuminate the reader's understanding. Each day will include a few steps to make the topics practical and applicable in modern life.

I encourage you to commit to reading and finishing this book in about four weeks. I suggest using Mondays through Fridays to read each chapter and Saturdays to review the previous chapters. Then, pick up the reading routine for the next five days until the twenty-one days of reading and reflection are done. Next, pick another book from the series and repeat the process. Read the next book and the next until you discover that you have spent almost a whole year learning about God and His ways!

You can repeat the process the following year by changing the order of books or passing your books to a family member. Incidentally, it is my experience that it is more fun and fulfilling to learn and grow with others. So, why don't you invite someone to read and discuss the topics as you grow together? I am optimistic that if you commit to the journey of becoming a *Daily Christian* for the next four weeks and beyond, it will transform your life from the inside out!

In this book, we will look at the role prayer plays in the life of a Christ follower. I know that most of us feel awkward when someone asks us about our prayer moments with God. We often feel like we may be praying wrong or not nearly long enough.

Rest assured, I will not spend your precious time trying to make you feel bad about your prayers to God. If anything, I want to make the prayer process as simple as possible so everyone can enjoy talking to the Lord. Prayer is supposed to liberate us and empower us to live life. Look at what the apostle Paul taught regarding prayer:

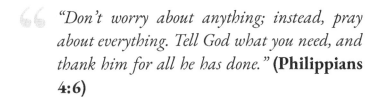

> *"Don't worry about anything; instead, pray about everything. Tell God what you need, and thank him for all he has done."* **(Philippians 4:6)**

You may respond, *"Well, how is that supposed to help me in my crazy, modern life?"*

Maybe this story from my own life could help you understand the simple power prayer brings to our stressed-out moments.

Recently my son drove back home from Los Angeles at a very late hour. As it got later and later, I felt stabs of anxiety in my stomach. *Where was he? Why wasn't he home yet? What is taking so long?*

I didn't want to call him because I wanted to instill in him that I trusted his driving skills. I knew he could get home without me riding shotgun on the phone. I knew that my concerns were a little irrational. When I was his age, I drove long distances by myself at night all the time without any problems. However, I also understood just how treacherous the freeways could get when you try to stay awake at the end of a long day. I was concerned that he might doze off somehow. It was getting even later, and I needed to go to bed. The next day was an early and busy one at work. What to do?

At that moment, I decided to transfer my concern to

Someone who could help me. I decided to pray and share my fears with Someone who was in the car with my son at that very moment. I'm talking about the One Who took care of me all my life and Someone who is all-knowing and all-powerful!

I pressed the *pause button* on all my anxious thoughts and prayed a short prayer. My prayer was nothing fancy. I asked God to protect my son as he drove home. I ended my prayer by thanking Him for hearing my prayer and for always being a good Father, not only to me but to my children as well. Peace settled where moments before, anxiety was upsetting my stomach. I promptly went to bed and fell soundly asleep.

At about 1:30 am, I woke up thirsty. As I padded to the bathroom for a drink of water, I noticed the hallway light shining. It was still on, as we left it when I went to bed. Instantly, anxious thoughts flooded my brain. Was my son home? I did not hear anything out there in his room. Was he still on his way? Did he get stuck by the roadside? I reached for the door handle to investigate... and then stopped myself.

Did I not ask the Lord for a safe journey for my son? Is God not able? I did not hear an incoming call asking for help, did I? I noticed my wife was blissfully asleep on her side of the bed. She seemed to be without a care. Why do I need confirmation right now? Why am I starting to freak out mentally?

At that moment, I made a decision. I resolutely turned back towards my bedside and slipped into the covers. As I closed my eyes, I whispered in my heart, *"I still trust you, Lord. I trusted you earlier when I went to bed, and I trust you now. Thank you for bringing my son home right on time."*

I woke up the next day and smiled when I looked out the window. My son's car was in front of our house, without any damage to the fenders! His bags and computer equipment were visible downstairs! *Yes! Thank you, God!*

I was so excited to connect with him when he finally came out of his room later that day. He told me that he had to stop somewhere along the way for a friend from his university. That's why he came home so late. He came home at about 1:30 am. The hall light I saw was on because he was still settling into his room.

I was glad I stopped myself from making that phone call the previous night. I was relieved that I paused my anxious thoughts long enough to pray. I was thankful that I could partner with God in a tense moment about the safety of a cherished son. I was so grateful that the Lord heard and answered my prayers.

The question is whether we will learn to include God in our life episodes filled with fearful emotions. Will I? Will you? Will we pause long enough to talk and listen to God? Will we reset our emotions and choose to keep our eyes on the Lord?

Many people, including Christians, do not seem to believe that prayer is essential. They would say that it is nice for others to pray for them, but they seldom pray for their situations until they get to the last desperate moments. If prayer were important in their lives, it would have been a daily priority and not merely an afterthought.

Sadly, many of us feel awkward and a little guilty whenever the topic of prayer comes up in conversation. Why would that be the case? I think it is because we know it should be a priority, but we often allow our busy lives to push prayer to the bottom of our to-do lists.

WHY PRAY?

Most of us don't like when somebody tells us to do anything. Think about it: We don't like it when someone tells us we need to exercise more or eat less fatty foods. We have difficulty listening to their input even when we know they are correct. We don't like it!

Regarding our spiritual well-being, allow me to get to the point: Whether you like it or not, we *must* pray!

In several of his letters to the early church, the apostle Paul wrote us that believers are to be in *continual prayer*[1]:

> *"Rejoice always, pray continually, give thanks in all circumstances; for this is God's will for you in Christ Jesus."* **(1 Thessalonians 5:16-18 NIV)**

He echoed what Jesus told His listeners years before, namely that believers should always pray and not lose heart:

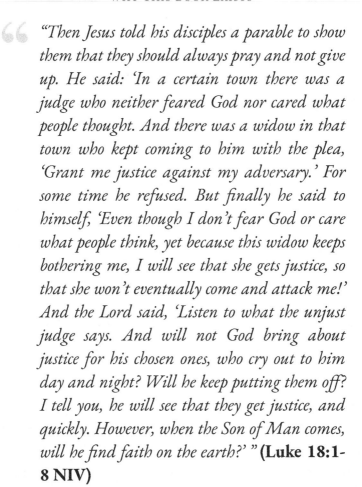

> *"Then Jesus told his disciples a parable to show them that they should always pray and not give up. He said: 'In a certain town there was a judge who neither feared God nor cared what people thought. And there was a widow in that town who kept coming to him with the plea, 'Grant me justice against my adversary.' For some time he refused. But finally he said to himself, 'Even though I don't fear God or care what people think, yet because this widow keeps bothering me, I will see that she gets justice, so that she won't eventually come and attack me!' And the Lord said, 'Listen to what the unjust judge says. And will not God bring about justice for his chosen ones, who cry out to him day and night? Will he keep putting them off? I tell you, he will see that they get justice, and quickly. However, when the Son of Man comes, will he find faith on the earth?'"* **(Luke 18:1-8 NIV)**

Realistically, for anyone to *always pray* and *not give up* requires great faith in God. In fact, it seems quite impossible, but the point is that prayer should be the first response, not the last resort in our lives. Jesus and Paul told us that prayer should be part of our lifestyles, not a rare event.

There are many reasons to pray. I have found that prayer will help me remain courageous as I face difficult circumstances. It helps me not to become discouraged in the face of opposition and seemingly insurmountable obstacles. Fundamentally, prayer changes us first, since you cannot encounter God in heartfelt conversation without being transformed from the inside out. Author Richard J. Foster does an excellent job explaining this reality[2]:

> "To pray is to change. Prayer is the central avenue God uses to transform us. If we are unwilling to change, we will abandon prayer as a noticeable characteristic of our lives."
>
> — RICHARD J. FOSTER

Not only do I change when I pray, but God gets the glory! Through prayer, we glorify and praise Him for all He is and has done for us (1 Thessalonians 5:18). Beyond that, prayer is very important to help us overcome life's many temptations. Jesus told Peter to pray to the Father for strength in overcoming the temptation of denying that he knew Jesus (Matthew 26:41).

A prayer for godly wisdom can help us when we have to make difficult decisions between competing options. Jesus exemplified the importance of prayer when He spent the night praying about who His disciples should be (Luke 6:12-13).

Prayer helps us to face and persevere in all kinds of

fierce struggles. Jesus clarified that we should bring our requests to our Heavenly Father:

> *"Ask and it will be given to you; seek and you will find; knock and the door will be opened to you."* (**Matthew 7:7 NIV**)

This scripture should not be misinterpreted by thinking that we *must* get everything we ask from God. When we ask for what is within the parameters of His will, He will have no problem giving those things to us at the right time:

> *"This is the confidence we have in approaching God: that if we ask anything according to his will, he hears us. And if we know that he hears us—whatever we ask—we know that we have what we asked of him."* (**1 John 5:14-15**)

Prayer is helpful when we struggle to discern God's will. Our example, Jesus, prayed daily to His Father for guidance and insight. We can expand our understanding of His will for us when we stay in regular communication with Him. More than that, prayer can help us obey the will of God daily.

Theologian and pastor R.C. Sproul asked, *"What is the goal of the Christian life?"* Here is his answer[3]:

> *"What is the goal of the Christian life? Godliness born of obedience to Christ. Obedience unlocks the riches of the Christian experience. Prayer is what prompts and nurtures obedience, putting the heart into the proper "frame of mind" to desire obedience."*

Obedience is so important! I don't always feel like obeying the Lord, but prayer helps me reach a place where I want to do what is right. It helps me to pray with Jesus, *"Father, not my will, but your will be done!"*

As you can see from the various Scripture references I mentioned here, prayer is not optional for the believer. Prayer is necessary because it connects us to God. Personal conversation and connection give us the supernatural power to obey the will of God!

Why another book on prayer? In this book, I hope to encourage you to lean into *lifestyle prayer* in a way that will benefit you now and in the future. I want people to see that prayer is simply communication with a loving God.

I have always felt saddened by the unnecessary guilt people seem to sense when the topic of prayer comes up in a conversation. They believe they will never be good enough and pray long enough to experience delight in talking to God. But talking to your heavenly Father should be a delight and something you can look forward to! Don't you agree?

For many believers, their prayer lives have become a

desolate battleground of personal failure. This is so unnecessary! A few slight adjustments can lift your chin as you look into the loving eyes of your heavenly Father!

I have compiled twenty-one principles in this book to help you enter this wide-open, expansive world of joyful prayer. For the next twenty-one days, do one thing extra every day as you journey through different instructions from the Bible. Resist the temptation to rush ahead and finish this book in a single setting. Instead, savor the day's lesson and allow yourself to ponder its implications. Then, the next day, you will not forget the previous day's lesson when you add a new strategy.

At first, it will feel like a new discipline, but you will quickly break through into pure delight. Sooner than you think, you will enjoy your prayer journey with God! Thank you for reading!

---

1. See also Philippians 4:6-7 and Ephesians 6:18-19.
2. Foster, Richard J. *The Celebration of Discipline: The Path To Spiritual Growth.* Harper & Row, 1988.
3. *The place of prayer by R.C. Sproul.* Ligonier Ministries. (n.d.). Retrieved September 21, 2022, from https://www.ligonier.org/learn/articles/place-prayer

Day 1
Prayer Is Simply Talking And Listening To God

> *"What a friend we have in Jesus, all our sins and griefs to bear! What a privilege to carry everything to God in prayer! O what peace we often forfeit, O what needless pain we bear, all because we do not carry everything to God in prayer.[1]"*
>
> — *Hymn lyrics by Joseph M. Scriven, 1820-1886*

FROM THE BEGINNING, God was close to mankind. He did not only shape and breathe into Adam but actively talked to him regularly. When Adam and Eve sinned in the garden of Eden, God came looking for them, calling out to re-establish the connection that was so precious to them. God wanted to talk about what went wrong and how they could go forward in the best possible way. God wanted to fix what broke their fellowship, and He took the initiative to seek out the fearful couple to bridge the gap caused by their disobedience.

Similarly, God wants to be in conversation with you, His most precious creation. Prayer is many things to many people, but it is important to know that it is a heartfelt and honest conversation between you and God. What is this conversation about?

JUST START
TALKING TO GOD ABOUT
YOUR FEARS, YOUR NEEDS,
AND YOUR DREAMS.

The conversation concerns what matters in your life and the Kingdom of God. You happen to live in a world

with specific limitations and have several unique needs as
you travel through your life. God cares about your life and
is waiting for you to open up communication channels.
Jesus makes it clear that God is waiting for you to start
talking, without hesitation, about what you need
from Him:

> "Don't bargain with God. Be direct. Ask for
> what you need. This isn't a cat-and-mouse,
> hide-and-seek game we're in. If your child asks
> for bread, do you trick him with sawdust? If he
> asks for fish, do you scare him with a live snake
> on his plate? As bad as you are, you wouldn't
> think of such a thing. You're at least decent to
> your own children. So don't you think the God
> who conceived you in love will be even better?"
> **(Matthew 7:7-11 MSG)**

Jesus made it crystal clear: Ask for what you need!
Would you try asking God for something you need
today, maybe even now? Remember that talking to God is
just like talking to your best friend... only much better!
Keep in mind that honest conversation is a two-way
street.

> "A man prayed, and at first he thought that
> prayer was talking. But he became more and
> more quiet until in the end he realized that
> prayer is listening.[2]"

— SOREN KIERKEGAARD

Don't just talk *at* God. Take a few moments to listen for His response within your heart. His response usually doesn't come to us as a booming voice reverberating off the walls. Instead, expect a whisper. You will know in your heart that it's His voice and not another.

God is willing and able to help you. Start talking to God about your fears, needs, and dreams. He is politely and patiently waiting for you.

Will you take the first step?

Then, are you willing to wait for His response... the whispers of His loving voice?

Keep in mind that prayer is simply talking and listening to God.

STUDY GUIDE:

1. What is the biggest challenge you face right now?
2. What are you most concerned about?
3. Could you write it down somewhere?
4. Take a few minutes to talk to God about the challenge you wrote down and ask for His help in specific ways.

5. Imagine asking Him like a little kid asking an adult for assistance with a difficult task.
6. You will be so glad you did!

REVIEW:

1. Prayer Is Simply Talking And Listening To God.

---

1. Kraby, Clayton. "Hymn Story: What a Friend We Have in Jesus." *ReasonableTheology.org*, 9 July 2022, https://reasonabletheology.org/hymn-story-friend-jesus/.
2. Administrator. "Voice of the Day: Kierkegaard on Prayer." *Sojourners*, 26 Nov. 2019, https://sojo.net/articles/voice-day-kierkegaard-prayer.

DAY 2
PRAYER SHOULD FLOW FROM A HUMBLE HEART

"*Have we trials and temptations? Is there trouble anywhere? We should never be discouraged; take it to the Lord in prayer. Can we find a friend so faithful, who will all our sorrows share? Jesus knows our every weakness; take it to the Lord in prayer.*[1]"

— HYMN LYRICS BY JOSEPH M. SCRIVEN,
1820-1886

"*Then if my people who are called by my name will humble themselves and pray and seek my face and turn from their wicked ways, I will hear from heaven and will forgive their sins and restore their land.*" **(2 Chronicles 7:14 NLT)**

WHILE IT IS true that we should feel comfortable in approaching God in prayer, we should also remember that God is holy and we are not. What exactly do I mean by *holy*?

To be holy means to be *exalted or worthy of complete devotion as one perfect in goodness and righteousness*[2].

That's who and what God is all the time. God is perfect in all His ways, and we, as humans, are flawed due to our limitations. We need His forgiveness regularly because our faults and flaws often separate us from God. However, our mistakes and sins are provided for in what Jesus had done for us in His death and resurrection. He paid the ultimate price to obtain the forgiveness we needed. As a result, we can approach God with humble confidence that we have been forgiven for what had once separated us from Him.

Jesus told a story of two men who approached God in prayer to teach His audience an important principle:

> *"To some who were confident of their own right-eousness and looked down on everyone else, Jesus told this parable: 'Two men went up to the temple to pray, one a Pharisee and the other a tax collector. The Pharisee stood by himself and prayed: 'God, I thank you that I am not like other people—robbers, evildoers, adulterers—or even like this tax collector. I fast twice a week and give a tenth of all I get.' But the tax collector stood at a distance. He would not even look up to heaven, but beat his breast and said, 'God, have mercy on me, a sinner.' I tell you that this man, rather than the other, went home justified before God. For all those who exalt themselves will be humbled, and those who humble themselves will be exalted.' "*
> **(Luke 18:9-14 NIV)**

The one man was superior in his attitude to the point of thanking God that he was not as bad as the other man next to him. The second man came with a broken and contrite heart, recognizing his frailties and sins in the presence of a holy God. Jesus taught that God heard the second man's humble prayers, while the prideful prayers of the first man went unanswered.

Today's chapter aims to remind you that we should

never have a superior or careless attitude when approaching God. He deserves our respect, reverence, and undivided attention. Check out what the prophet Isaiah wrote about people who come to God with a humble and contrite heart:

> "The high and lofty one who lives in eternity, the Holy One, says this: 'I live in the high and holy place with those whose spirits are <u>contrite and humble</u>. I restore the crushed spirit of the <u>humble</u> and revive the courage of those with <u>repentant hearts</u>.' " **(Isaiah 57:15 NLT)** (Emphases mine)

God wants to restore whatever may be lacking in your life. He wants to revive your weary soul, but we all must come to Him with contrite and humble hearts.

~

STUDY GUIDE:

1. Can you think of a time when you talked to God with a flippant attitude? Maybe you were not paying attention or giving God your full attention as you spoke to Him.

2. Can you see from the scriptures above that God rewards those who approach Him with the proper respect and awe?

3. Let's agree that from now on, we will talk to God, but we will make sure to pay our respects and give attention to how we speak to Him.

4. Remind yourself that the appropriate attitude is essential to God.

REVIEW:

1. Prayer Is Simply Talking And Listening To God.
2. Prayer Should Flow From A Humble Heart.

---

1. Kraby, Clayton. "Hymn Story: What a Friend We Have in Jesus." *ReasonableTheology.org*, 9 July 2022, https://reasonabletheology.org/hymn-story-friend-jesus/.
2. "Holy Definition & Meaning." *Merriam-Webster*, Merriam-Webster, https://www.merriam-webster.com/dictionary/holy.

DAY 3
YOUR PRAYERS SHOULD BE CONFIDENT

> "So let us come <u>boldly</u> to the throne of our gracious God. There we will receive his mercy, and we will find grace to help us when we need it most." **(Hebrews 4:16 NLT)**(Emphasis mine)

YOU MUST BE confident in the goodness of God. If God is a good God, which He is, and if He cares deeply about us, which He does, why would He not receive us as we humbly approach His throne? Why would you expect anything less than a positive reception and a generous response from a good God?

The scripture above clarifies that a bold or confident conversation with God will result in mercy and grace. This means that confident prayer will have amazing results!

Jesus taught His disciples that they could expect joy as a result of their prayers to God the Father:

"You haven't done this before. Ask, using my name, and you will receive, and you will have abundant joy." **(John 16:24 NLT)**

We should be excited to talk to God, and we can have high expectations about the results of our prayers! God loves to see us approach Him with confidence that He will receive us favorably because it shows that we think He is a good Father!

Remember the following scripture from our first day of prayer:

 "You're at least decent to your own children. So don't you think the God who conceived you in love will be even better?" **(Matthew 7:11 MSG)**

Your prayers should be confident!

∿

STUDY GUIDE:

1. When you pray, bring your requests to God's throne with new confidence in His goodness.
2. Believe in His eternal willingness to give you what you need today.
3. What new items would you add to your prayer requests if you knew God was willing to assist you?
4. Go ahead and take a moment to bring some new items to God as you approach Him confidently.

REVIEW:

1. Prayer Is Simply Talking And Listening To God.
2. Prayer Should Flow From A Humble Heart.
3. Your Prayers Should Be Confident.

DAY 4
YOUR PRAYERS SHOULD BE CONCISE AND TO THE POINT

> *"When you pray, don't babble on and on as people of other religions do. <u>They think their prayers are answered merely by repeating their words repeatedly. Don't be like them,</u> for your Father knows exactly what you need before you ask him."* **(Matthew 6:7-8 NLT)***(Emphasis mine)*

IN DEALING WITH PEOPLE, we often have to repeat ourselves to be understood. However, in prayer, you must get to the point and talk to God like He already knows what you need. Your objective in prayer is to invite Him into your situation and trust Him. You are not trying to *inform* God. No, you are *inviting and including* Him.

Make a point of not saying the same thing over and over. Once you earn this simple principle, you will discover it is liberating. It will require some self-awareness and self-discipline on your part at first, but that is a good thing. Your prayer times will become more effective and meaningful.

Think about it: You would not want to ramble on and on if you should get a chance to speak to the president of the United States, would you? So why ramble on when speaking to God, the Ruler of the Universe?

Get to the point. Could you keep it simple? God is more intelligent than you will ever know, and He is ready to help you.

STUDY GUIDE:

1. Present your requests to the Lord today.
2. Make sure you do not allow useless repetitions in your conversation with Him.
3. He already knows what you need and wants you to verbalize it simply to show your faith and dependence on Him.

REVIEW:

1. Prayer Is Simply Talking And Listening To God.
2. Prayer Should Flow From A Humble Heart.
3. Your Prayers Should Be Confident.
4. Your Prayers Should Be Concise And To The Point.

DAY 5
YOUR PRAYERS SHOULD BE CONSISTENT AND CONSTANT

> *"Never stop praying."* **(1 Thessalonians 5:17 NLT)**

THROUGHOUT HISTORY, men and women have prayed to God in all kinds of situations. Being omnipresent and omniscient, God is always near and knows how to help us. There is no circumstance or situation where we should allow ourselves to believe that we cannot talk to God.

Daniel prayed on the way to the lion's den, and God shut the mouths of the lions. Moses talked to God on the shores of the Red Sea, and God parted the waters right on time. Whether in good times or bad times, lean times or abundant times, early in the morning or late at night... talking to God is not only possible but critical to our survival!

Simply put, we need to talk to God at all hours and on all occasions!

Sometimes I feel like God may not want to talk to me because I messed up or had a bad attitude. Yet, that is precisely when I need to speak to God the most!

Please hear this today: Talk to God consistently in that you do not let a day pass without having been in conversation with Him. Talk to God constantly in that you bring

Him into every significant or mundane moment of your day. Your prayers should be consistent and constant!

Study Guide:

1. See if you can remember to talk to God throughout today.
2. As you drive, work, and get ready to eat... include God by talking to Him.
3. Remind yourself and others that He loves to hear from us!

Review:

1. Prayer Is Simply Talking And Listening To God.
2. Prayer Should Flow From A Humble Heart.
3. Your Prayers Should Be Confident.
4. Your Prayers Should Be Concise And To The Point.
5. Your Prayers Should Be Consistent And Constant.

DAY 6
PRAY IN JESUS' NAME

> *"You didn't choose me. I chose you. I appointed you to go and produce lasting fruit, so that the Father will give you whatever you ask for, <u>using my name</u>."* **(John 15:16 NLT)** *(Emphasis mine)*

> *"At that time you won't need to ask me for anything. I tell you the truth, you will ask the Father directly, and <u>he will grant your request because you use my name</u>."* **(John 16:23 NLT)***(Emphasis mine)*

HERE WE HAVE the words of Jesus, and He tells us that we are to produce good fruit, or good results, as we live here on the earth. He also tells us that we can ask for what we need directly from the Father and that we will get what we need. Why? Because we present our needs in the name of Jesus.

It is not as if the words *"in the name of Jesus"* provide magical powers to our prayers. It is not as if we can say the phrase at the end of a prayer, and then God will be obligated to do whatever we ask.

We must understand that praying for things that agree with God's will is the essence of praying in Jesus' name.

In other words, praying in Jesus' name means the same thing as praying according to the will of God:

> *"And we are confident that <u>he hears us when-</u>
> <u>ever we ask for anything that pleases him</u>. And
> since we know he hears us when we make our
> requests, we also know that <u>he will give us what</u>
> <u>we ask for</u>."* (**1 John 5:14-15 NLT**)
> *(Emphases mine)*

Praying in Jesus' name is praying for things that will honor and glorify Jesus. When we ask in the name of Jesus, it means that our prayers will be accepted in the same way a prayer from Jesus Himself would have been accepted!

That is pretty amazing! Don't you agree?

Doesn't that give you more confidence for your prayers to be answered? It is sad to see Christians without the help they need because they have not read or understood these powerful promises! It is right there, within reach, if only they will read it, believe it, and act on it.

The question is... will *you*?

STUDY GUIDE:

1. Go ahead and talk to God about your needs and concerns. Don't forget to end your prayer time by stating that you ask these things in the name of Jesus.

2. When you ask in the name of Jesus, according to the will of God, the Father wants to bless your request with a resounding *"Yes!"*

REVIEW:

1. Prayer Is Simply Talking And Listening To God.
2. Prayer Should Flow From A Humble Heart.
3. Your Prayers Should Be Confident.
4. Your Prayers Should Be Concise And To The Point.
5. Your Prayers Should Be Consistent And Constant.
6. Pray In Jesus' Name.

DAY 7
PRAY ABOUT EVERYTHING

" *"Are we weak and heavy laden, cumbered with a load of care? Precious Savior, still our refuge; take it to the Lord in prayer. Do thy friends despise, forsake thee? Take it to the Lord in prayer! In his arms he'll take and shield thee; thou wilt find a solace there.*[1] *"*

— HYMN LYRICS BY JOSEPH M. SCRIVEN, 1820-1886

" *"Don't worry about anything; instead, pray about everything. Tell God what you need, and thank him for all he has done. Then you will experience God's peace, which exceeds anything we can understand. His peace will guard your hearts and minds as you live in Christ Jesus."* **(Philippians 4:6-7 NLT)***(Emphasis mine)*

have to waste one minute worrying and being anxious! Instead, we are told to go and talk to God about all the things that concern us. We are instructed to tell God what we need and to thank Him for everything He has done.

I experience that great peace usually follows such an exchange with God. In a moment, that peace wraps itself around my thoughts and emotions, and I am more than able to face my day.

How is that possible? Think about it: I gave God my concerns, and He gave me His reassuring Presence. What an exchange! When I commit to recalling all the wonderful and miraculous things the Lord had done for me, I cannot help but feel satisfied and motivated. Now I am ready to conquer the challenges in my day!

It is hard to be a pessimist when you have a grateful heart!

Pray about everything!

STUDY GUIDE:

1. Are you feeling a little anxious today? Pray about it!
2. Tell God what you need.
3. Take time to thank Him for what He has done and is about to do.
4. Get ready for God's incredible peace!

REVIEW:

1. Prayer Is Simply Talking And Listening To God.
2. Prayer Should Flow From A Humble Heart.
3. Your Prayers Should Be Confident.
4. Your Prayers Should Be Concise And To The Point.
5. Your Prayers Should Be Consistent And Constant.
6. Pray In Jesus' Name.
7. Pray About Everything!

---

1. Kraby, Clayton. "Hymn Story: What a Friend We Have in Jesus." *ReasonableTheology.org*, 9 July 2022, https://reasonabletheology.org/hymn-story-friend-jesus/.

DAY 8

YOU DO NOT HAVE BECAUSE YOU DON'T ASK GOD

" *"What is causing the quarrels and fights among you? Don't they come from the evil desires at war within you? You want what you don't have, so you scheme and kill to get it. You are jealous of what others have, but you can't get it, so you fight and wage war to take it away from them. Yet <u>you don't have what you want because you don't ask God for it</u>."* **(James 4:1-2 NLT)***(Emphasis mine)*

HOW CAN it be so simple? All we have to do is ask God? I thought we all have to go out and compete and fight and claw our way over others until we finally can earn what we need. At least, that's what this world wants us to believe as we fight each other for limited opportunities and resources.

But there seems to be a better way in God's Kingdom. God has no scarcity in His warehouses; whatever is missing, He can create or summon with a whisper.

He can produce it from a rock or multiply a little boy's lunch to feed a multitude.

Maybe it is because we see other people, our jobs, our environment, or our country as our sources. Yet, when those supposed sources fail, which they eventually will, we begin to scheme, fight, fuss and claw.

All we have to do, though, is go to our only trustworthy Source, God, in prayer, asking Him for what we need! Then these other sources will line up as God helps us.

Remember what Jesus taught in the Gospel of Matthew:

> *"Therefore do not worry, saying, 'What shall we eat?' or 'What shall we drink?' or 'What shall we wear?' For after all these things the Gentiles seek. For your heavenly Father knows that you need all these things. But seek first the kingdom of God and His righteousness, and all these things shall be added to you."* **(Matthew 6:31-33 NIV)**

Study Guide:

1. What is it you think you need?
2. Have you fallen into the common trap of looking to people to give it to you?
3. If you don't have it yet, have you asked God for it?
4. Ask Him now.

Review:

1. Prayer Is Simply Talking And Listening To God.
2. Prayer Should Flow From A Humble Heart.
3. Your Prayers Should Be Confident.
4. Your Prayers Should Be Concise And To The Point.
5. Your Prayers Should Be Consistent And Constant.

6. Pray In Jesus' Name.
7. Pray About Everything!
8. You Do Not Have Because You Don't Ask God.

DAY 9
ASKING GOD WITH THE WRONG MOTIVE DOESN'T WORK

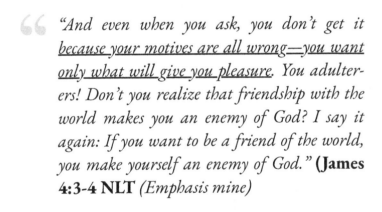

"And even when you ask, you don't get it <u>because your motives are all wrong—you want only what will give you pleasure.</u> You adulterers! Don't you realize that friendship with the world makes you an enemy of God? I say it again: If you want to be a friend of the world, you make yourself an enemy of God." **(James 4:3-4 NLT** *(Emphasis mine)*

WE MUST all realize that our God does not sponsor selfish pursuits or self-indulgent pleasures. Heavenly Father wants to see us move beyond being carnal and selfish to mature into living selfless lives of service. While He does not deny us our basic human needs of food, shelter, and clothing, He does not want us to be involved in trivial pursuits. The things of this world should become less and less critical, and the quest for God's Kingdom should become our own.

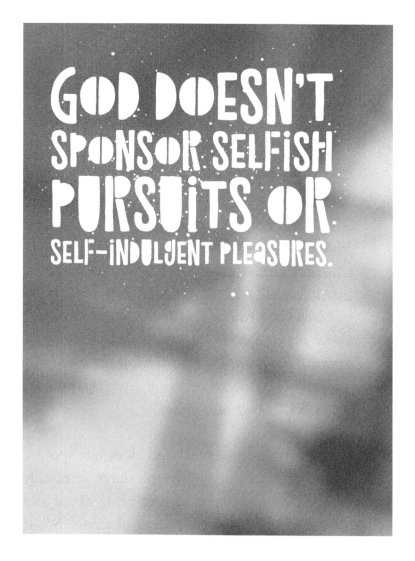

The quest of the Kingdom is to bring glory to the King by loving Him and loving people. It is not about loving our pleasure but serving our neighbors in the name of the Lord. Our desire should be to share His Good News and eternal love with everyone.

Consider your recent talks with the Lord. Were you more focused on your wants and pleasures or your actual needs as a child in God's Kingdom? Again, there are wants and needs... and the mature believer can discern the difference.

God loves us, and He does not mind providing the occasional treat. Yet, our prayers should flow from a pure motivation to be about our Heavenly Father's business here on Earth.

We are on the earth, but we are not of this earth, and earthly pleasures should not dominate our conversations with the Lord.

STUDY GUIDE:

1. Consider your recent prayer requests.
2. How many of them could be considered selfish requests to indulge in earthly pleasures?
3. How many requests truly reflect the Kingdom priorities you learn about in Scripture?
4. Let's commit to recalibrating our motivations in prayer.

5. May our motivations more accurately reflect
   what God would consider mature and
   pleasing in His sight.

REVIEW:

1. Prayer Is Simply Talking And Listening
   To God.
2. Prayer Should Flow From A Humble Heart.
3. Your Prayers Should Be Confident.
4. Your Prayers Should Be Concise And To The
   Point.
5. Your Prayers Should Be Consistent And
   Constant.
6. Pray In Jesus' Name.
7. Pray About Everything!
8. You Do Not Have Because You Don't
   Ask God.
9. Asking God With The Wrong Motive Doesn't
   Work.

Day 10
Ask Expecting To Receive From God

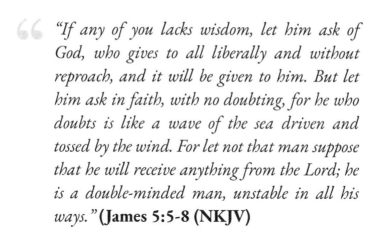

"If any of you lacks wisdom, let him ask of God, who gives to all liberally and without reproach, and it will be given to him. But let him ask in faith, with no doubting, for he who doubts is like a wave of the sea driven and tossed by the wind. For let not that man suppose that he will receive anything from the Lord; he is a double-minded man, unstable in all his ways." **(James 5:5-8 (NKJV)**

IT IS essential to have high expectations of God when we pray. To doubt God's willingness to give to us is to weaken our prayers. God loves to share with lavish generosity, and He loves to hear us asking Him in faith.

Our part is to ask without doubt, and His part is to give to us abundantly according to His will. A doubting prayer cannot succeed because God expects us to be fully persuaded that He is willing and able to provide for us.

Abraham understood this principle, and he received miraculous outcomes because of his faith-filled prayers:

"Even when there was no reason for hope, Abraham kept hoping—believing that he would become the father of many nations. For God had said to him, 'That's how many descendants you will have!' And Abraham's faith did not weaken, even though, at about 100 years of age, he figured his body was as good as dead—and so was Sarah's womb. Abraham never wavered in believing God's promise. In fact, his faith grew stronger, and in this he brought glory to God. He was fully convinced that God can do whatever he promises." **(Romans 4:18-21 NLT)**

Like Abraham, we must be fully convinced that God can do whatever He promises! He is still a miracle-working God, and He expects us to have high expectations when we present our requests to Him in prayer.

STUDY GUIDE:

1. Have you ever asked God for something while doubting whether He would answer your prayers?

2. Are you fully convinced that God is not only able but willing to do what you have asked Him to do?

3. Make this declaration today as you pray:

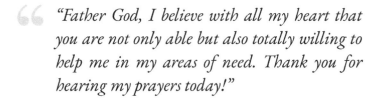 *"Father God, I believe with all my heart that you are not only able but also totally willing to help me in my areas of need. Thank you for hearing my prayers today!"*

REVIEW:

1. Prayer Is Simply Talking And Listening To God.
2. Prayer Should Flow From A Humble Heart.
3. Your Prayers Should Be Confident.
4. Your Prayers Should Be Concise And To The Point.
5. Your Prayers Should Be Consistent And Constant.
6. Pray In Jesus' Name.
7. Pray About Everything!
8. You Do Not Have Because You Don't Ask God.
9. Asking God With The Wrong Motive Doesn't Work.
10. Ask Expecting To Receive From God.

DAY 11
ASK GOD TO BLESS YOUR ENEMIES AS YOU PRAY

> *"You have heard the law that says, 'Love your neighbor' and hate your enemy. But I say, love your enemies! <u>Pray for those who persecute you!</u> In that way, you will be acting as true children of your Father in heaven."* **(Matthew 5:43-45 NLT)***(Emphasis mine)*

> *"<u>Bless those who persecute you.</u> Don't curse them; pray that God will bless them."* **(Romans 12:14 NLT)***(Emphasis mine)*

> *"The eyes of the Lord watch over <u>those who do right,</u> and <u>his ears are open to their prayers."</u>* **(1 Peter 3:12 NLT** *(Emphases mine)*

TO PRAY for those who persecute you is not easy for anyone. The most natural thing is to hurl insults at them and to talk to God about *fixing them good!* However, Jesus introduced a higher standard and called us to act as true children of our Father in Heaven!

Just when you think that you have figured prayer out, you are getting challenged to a higher level of praying. But praying for our enemies? That seems almost unthinkable!

Yet, there is a promise in our scriptures we should not treat lightly. Peter writes in his letter that God's ears are mainly open, or receptive, to the requests of people who do right.

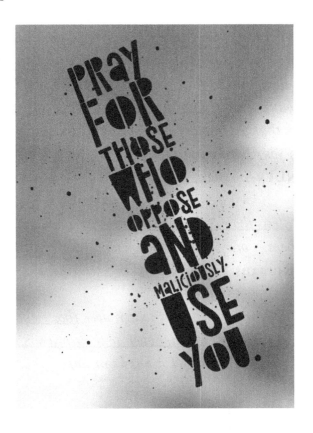

Do you want the Lord to hear your requests? Do what is right. What is right is to pray for your enemies, especially when it hurts the most. This kind of prayer gets the Father's attention.

Jesus is our example in praying for our enemies. He was on the cross, and, after hours of intense suffering and torture, with some of His last strength, He made an effort to pray for His enemies:

> "Jesus said, 'Father, forgive them, for they don't know what they are doing.'" **(Luke 23:24 NLT)**

Stephen, the first Christian martyr, followed in Jesus' footsteps by praying for his enemies:

> "As they stoned him, Stephen prayed, 'Lord Jesus, receive my spirit.' He fell to his knees, shouting, 'Lord, don't charge them with this sin!' And with that, he died." **(Acts 7:59-60 NLT)**(Emphasis mine)

We are all called to pray for those who oppose us and despitefully use us in life. This way, we imitate Jesus and show that our Father is in Heaven.

Remember to ask God to bless your enemies when you pray.

STUDY GUIDE:

1. Think of someone who has caused you great harm, grief, or pain.
2. Now ask God to bless that person and to forgive their offense against you.
3. This will liberate you and liberate them!

REVIEW:

1. Prayer Is Simply Talking And Listening To God.
2. Prayer Should Flow From A Humble Heart.
3. Your Prayers Should Be Confident.
4. Your Prayers Should Be Concise And To The Point.
5. Your Prayers Should Be Consistent And Constant.
6. Pray In Jesus' Name.
7. Pray About Everything!
8. You Do Not Have Because You Don't Ask God.
9. Asking God With The Wrong Motive Doesn't Work.
10. Ask Expecting To Receive From God.
11. Ask God To Bless Your Enemies As You Pray.

DAY 12

ASK THE LORD TO MAKE YOU MORE LOVING

"*When I think of all this, I fall to my knees and pray to the Father, the Creator of everything in heaven and on earth. I pray that from his glorious, unlimited resources he will empower you with inner strength through his Spirit. Then Christ will make his home in your hearts as you trust in him. Your roots will grow down into God's love and keep you strong. And may you have the power to understand, as all God's people should, how wide, how long, how high, and how deep his love is. May you experience the love of Christ, though it is too great to understand fully. Then you will be made complete with all the fullness of life and power that comes from God.*" **(Ephesians 3:14-19 NLT)***(Emphasis mine)*

PAUL THE APOSTLE prayed that the Ephesian believers would understand the kind of love we are called to extend to others: the *God kind* of love. God's love is wider, higher, and more profound than we can ever truly comprehend, and it is critical to our daily lives.

In his letter to the believers at Corinth, the apostle tried to define what this love looks like and how it is supposed to operate through our lives:

> *"Love is patient and kind. Love is not jealous or boastful or proud or rude. It does not demand its own way. It is not irritable, and it keeps no record of being wronged. It does not rejoice about injustice but rejoices whenever the truth wins out. Love never gives up, never loses faith, is always hopeful, and endures through every circumstance."* **(1 Corinthians 13:4-7 NLT)**

Now, if you personalize this scripture, you may want to pray:

> *"Dear Lord, please help me to become more patient and kind. Please help me not to be jealous or boastful or proud or rude. Please help me not to demand my way, and help me not be irritable. Please help me not to keep a record of being wronged by others! Please help me to rejoice whenever the truth wins out and never to rejoice over injustice. Please help me never to give up, never lose faith, and to be always hopeful, enduring through every circumstance that may come my way!"*

Ask the Lord to make you more loving. This is the kind of prayer God loves to answer!

STUDY GUIDE:

1. Looking at our scriptures today, would you agree that you may need to mature into the kind of love God wants to release through you?
2. Or, do you think you have *"arrived?"*
3. Do you agree that the Lord of love will have to help you to become a more loving person?
4. Regularly ask the Lord to make you more loving.

REVIEW:

1. Prayer Is Simply Talking And Listening To God.
2. Prayer Should Flow From A Humble Heart.
3. Your Prayers Should Be Confident.
4. Your Prayers Should Be Concise And To The Point.
5. Your Prayers Should Be Consistent And Constant.
6. Pray In Jesus' Name.

7. Pray About Everything!
8. You Do Not Have Because You Don't Ask God.
9. Asking God With The Wrong Motive Doesn't Work.
10. Ask Expecting To Receive From God.
11. Ask God To Bless Your Enemies As You Pray.
12. Ask The Lord To Make You More Loving As You Pray.

DAY 13
MAKE TALKING TO GOD A PRIORITY
EVERY DAY

> *"But I will call on God, and the Lord will rescue me. Morning, noon, and night I cry out in my distress, and the Lord hears my voice. He ransoms me and keeps me safe from the battle waged against me, though many still oppose me. God, who has ruled forever, will hear me and humble them."* **(Psalm 55: 17-19 NLT)** *(Emphases mine)*

> *"O Lord, God of my salvation, I cry out to you by day. I come to you at night. Now hear my prayer; listen to my cry."* **(Psalm 88:1-2 NLT)** *(Emphases mine)*

KING DAVID and Heman the Ezrahite wrote these two portions of scripture to show that they prioritized prayer

in their lives. In the middle of their distressing circumstances, they made the time to meet with God and let Him
know they needed help.

We are tempted to get so engaged with problem-
solving and putting out fires that we forget to invite God
into our situations. Urgent things demand our immediate
attention. We go into crisis mode, which exposes us to the
risk of making ill-advised decisions. We especially need
divine intervention amid our crises.

If we have not already established the discipline of
meeting with the Lord daily, we may get disconnected
from our Heavenly Father when the bad times hit. Talking
to God must become a priority. Unless we schedule our
prayer priorities, they will be supplanted by other urgent
but less important things.

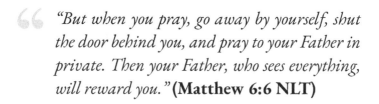

*"But when you pray, go away by yourself, shut
the door behind you, and pray to your Father in
private. Then your Father, who sees everything,
will reward you."* **(Matthew 6:6 NLT)**

If you don't schedule a regular *"when,"* you cannot
expect to have the frequent rewards of answered prayers.
My wife and I have three boys, and I used to drive them to
school early in the morning. I always prayed for us all as
we drove out of the driveway. I pray before every meal
with my family.

I made it a habit to walk into my children's rooms at

night to pray with them. We thanked God for the day and asked Him for His protection during the night. I prioritized and scheduled the *when* so that it may become normalized in our family's lifestyle.

Prayer should be a priority, and it only becomes a lifestyle when we schedule times of prayer at the intersections of our days.

STUDY GUIDE:

1. Have you made talking to God a priority in your life?
2. Do you have scheduled times of prayer?
3. How can you schedule times of prayer in the future?

REVIEW:

1. Prayer Is Simply Talking And Listening To God.
2. Prayer Should Flow From A Humble Heart.
3. Your Prayers Should Be Confident.
4. Your Prayers Should Be Concise And To The Point.
5. Your Prayers Should Be Consistent And Constant.
6. Pray In Jesus' Name.
7. Pray About Everything!
8. You Do Not Have Because You Don't Ask God.
9. Asking God With The Wrong Motive Doesn't Work.

10. Ask Expecting To Receive From God.
11. Ask God To Bless Your Enemies As You Pray.
12. Ask The Lord To Make You More Loving As You Pray.
13. Make Talking To God A Priority Every Day.

DAY 14
PRAY ACCORDING TO GOD'S WILL

> *"And we are confident that <u>he hears us when-ever we ask for anything that pleases him</u>. And since we know he hears us when we make our requests, we also know that he will give us what we ask for."* **(1 John 5:14-15 NLT)** *(Emphasis mine)*

JESUS UNDERSTOOD the importance of doing the Father's will. He shaped His life and ministry around pleasing God by obeying His will. God is not obligated to sponsor anyone who contradicts His will and values.

> *"For I have come down from heaven to <u>do the will of God</u> who sent me, <u>not to do my own will</u>."* **(John 6:38 NLT)** *(Emphases mine)*

> *"Father, if you are willing, please take this cup of suffering away from me. Yet <u>I want your will to be done, not mine.</u>"* **(Luke 22:42 NLT)** *(Emphasis mine)*

The will of God is revealed in the pages of the Bible. We must bring our requests to God with a sincere attitude of total submission to God's will. Years ago, there was an old television show called *Father Knows Best*. We must remind ourselves that we live the best possible lives when we desire to know and do God's will. Our Heavenly Father knows best!

Knowing God's will before we pray will require investing time in reading the Bible. Scripture teaches us about God's will and ways. We must try to understand what He values and considers worthy of His time and resources.

God has priorities and gladly supplies us with what we need to fulfill our Kingdom responsibilities. Again, He is not obligated to sponsor and provide us with trivial things to satisfy our quest for more and more selfish pleasure.

> *"And even when you ask, you don't get it because your motives are all wrong—<u>you want only what will give you pleasure.</u> You adulterers! Don't you realize that friendship with the world makes you an enemy of God? I say it again: If you want to be a friend of the world,*

you make yourself an enemy of God.” **(James 4:3-4 NLT)***(Emphasis mine)*

Spend the time to find out what God wants from us, as revealed in the Bible. When you ask according to the will of God, He delights in granting your requests.

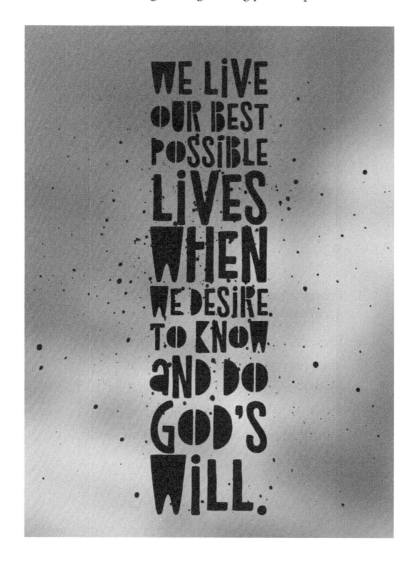

STUDY GUIDE:

1. Look at the things you have been asking God for lately.
2. Do they contradict or confirm the values and will of God as revealed in scripture?
3. In your prayer time, remind yourself of what you have read in the Bible concerning your needs.
4. Remind yourself what God had promised you in Scripture.
5. It will build your faith and give you the confidence to ask God according to His will, not just your desire.

REVIEW:

1. Prayer Is Simply Talking And Listening To God.
2. Prayer Should Flow From A Humble Heart.
3. Your Prayers Should Be Confident.
4. Your Prayers Should Be Concise And To The Point.
5. Your Prayers Should Be Consistent And Constant.
6. Pray In Jesus' Name.
7. Pray About Everything!

8. You Do Not Have Because You Don't Ask God.
9. Asking God With The Wrong Motive Doesn't Work.
10. Ask Expecting To Receive From God.
11. Ask God To Bless Your Enemies As You Pray.
12. Ask The Lord To Make You More Loving As You Pray.
13. Make Talking To God A Priority Every Day.
14. Pray According To God's Will.

DAY 15
PRAYER FRAMES HELP SHAPE OUR PRAYERS

> *"In this manner, therefore, pray: Our Father in heaven, hallowed be Your name. Your kingdom come. Your will be done on earth as it is in heaven. Give us this day our daily bread. And forgive us our debts, as we forgive our debtors. And do not lead us into temptation, but deliver us from the evil one. For Yours is the kingdom and the power and the glory forever. Amen."* **(Matthew 6:9-13 NKJV)**

JESUS GAVE HIS FOLLOWERS THIS "FRAMEWORK" for prayer to assist them in their prayer lives. His intent was not necessarily to provide them with a *form prayer* to memorize and recite, as many believers now do. Instead, it was to give a prayer framework to help His followers have meaningful, heartfelt talks with God. The Lord's Prayer is a guideline for prayer that can help us cover what is most important as we talk to God.

> *"All praying starts with forms of prayer... yet relationships don't thrive on rigid communication. Relationships require originality and spontaneity."*
>
> — SAMUEL CHADWICK, 1860–1932

As you look at the Lord's Prayer as a framework, you see that we should approach God with a respectful appreciation of His holiness. Right away, it is important to seek His will, not our own. Then, bringing our daily needs and requests to Him is appropriate.

As we ask for the forgiveness of our sins, we acknowledge that we are required to forgive others as we receive forgiveness ourselves. Finally, we ask for God's protection from temptation and the evil that lurks in our fallen world. Then, we end by reaffirming God as King of our universe by saying, *"For thine is the kingdom, and the power, and the glory, for ever and ever. Amen."*

In a typical cement project, the workers lay the framework with wooden planks in the desired shape. Next, the cement truck is called in to fill the frame with cement. After the cement had dried, the framework of planks needs to be removed. This is how you form what you desire to establish, whether it be a patio, a driveway, or the foundation of a house.

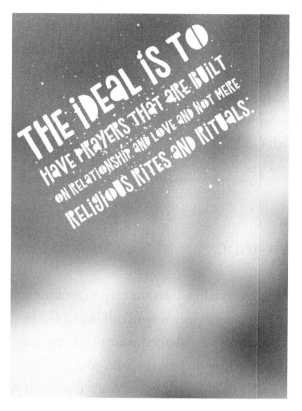

THE IDEAL IS TO HAVE PRAYERS THAT ARE BUILT ON RELATIONSHIP AND LOVE AND NOT MERE RELIGIOUS RITES AND RITUALS.

Similarly, the *form prayer* helps you shape your prayer time, and you fill it with your own words. After doing that for a while, you can remove the prayer frame because it has served its purpose: to shape and establish your prayer life.

The prayer frame should never replace your heartfelt prayer times with God. After a house is built, the builders remove the scaffolding—the same with prayer frames.

We should use prayer outlines (there are many helpful prayer outlines and frameworks available) to keep in mind how to approach God and what to cover. After you are well established in prayer, you should use your uniqueness in talking to God. The idea is to have prayers built on relationships and love, not just religious rites and rituals.

The prayer form gives you the confidence to start. After a while, the relationship you have established gives you the confidence to build and comfortably share your heart with God.

STUDY GUIDE:

1. Have you fallen into the trap of making form prayers your only way of talking to God?
2. Once you have shaped your prayer time and learned how to pray, expand your time with God by adding relational conversation in your prayer times.
3. Honesty and transparency will assist you in this regard.

REVIEW:

1. Prayer Is Simply Talking And Listening To God.
2. Prayer Should Flow From A Humble Heart.
3. Your Prayers Should Be Confident.
4. Your Prayers Should Be Concise And To The Point.

5. Your Prayers Should Be Consistent And Constant.
6. Pray In Jesus' Name.
7. Pray About Everything!
8. You Do Not Have Because You Don't Ask God.
9. Asking God With The Wrong Motive Doesn't Work.
10. Ask Expecting To Receive From God.
11. Ask God To Bless Your Enemies As You Pray.
12. Ask The Lord To Make You More Loving As You Pray.
13. Make Talking To God A Priority Every Day.
14. Pray According To God's Will.
15. Prayer Frames Help Shape Our Prayers.

DAY 16
ASK GOD TO CHANGE THE WAY YOU THINK

> *"Don't copy the behavior and customs of this world, but <u>let God transform you into a new person by changing the way you think</u>. Then you will learn to know God's will for you, which is good and pleasing and perfect."* **(Romans 12:2 NLT)***(Emphasis mine)*

MANY PEOPLE in our world do not take the time to speak to God or to believe in God for great things. They are hostile, pessimistic, and toxic in their thinking, which shows in everything they do. As believers, our challenge is that we don't always realize to what degree this world has affected our thinking.

Fear, doubt, and unbelief may have entered our thinking patterns. It can become challenging for us to pray prayers aligned with the *"good and pleasing and perfect will of God"* for us. We sometimes struggle to pray for

God's intervention and provision. Unknowingly, we have defaulted to the world's way of negative thinking.

> *"So then faith comes by hearing, and hearing by the word of God."* **(Romans 10:17 NKJV)**

We must ask the Lord to help us as we retrain our minds by reading the Bible to think more like King's kids rather than outcasts and rebels. When we read the Bible, we become acquainted with the ways of God and the will of God. This way, we are better equipped to pray according to God's revealed will.

We have learned in this series of teachings that God answers prayers that align with His will. This retraining of our minds will make us become new persons God can use in a mighty way.

Make it a priority to pray daily so God may help you change your thoughts about your life, your family, and others. You will be so glad you did!

STUDY GUIDE:

1. Take a moment to inventory how you have been thinking about your most significant challenges lately. Were you positive that God is helping you to overcome, or were you negative, assuming that all is lost and beyond repair?

2. Ask God to show you in the Word how He wants to be your Good Shepherd, guarding, guiding, and providing for you.

3. Now pray and ask the Lord to help you by changing your thinking from tragedy to triumph, defeat to victory, and negative to positive.

4. Take a moment to thank God for helping you with your thoughts.

5. Your prayer outcomes will change for the better when you leave the world's way of thinking behind.

REVIEW:

1. Prayer Is Simply Talking And Listening To God.

2. Prayer Should Flow From A Humble Heart.

3. Your Prayers Should Be Confident.

4. Your Prayers Should Be Concise And To The Point.

5. Your Prayers Should Be Consistent And Constant.

6. Pray In Jesus' Name.

7. Pray About Everything!

8. You Do Not Have Because You Don't Ask God.

9. Asking God With The Wrong Motive Doesn't Work.

10. Ask Expecting To Receive From God.
11. Ask God To Bless Your Enemies As You Pray.
12. Ask The Lord To Make You More Loving As You Pray.
13. Make Talking To God A Priority Every Day.
14. Pray According To God's Will.
15. Prayer Frames Help Shape Our Prayers.
16. Ask God To Change The Way You Think.

DAY 17
THINK AT A HIGHER LEVEL WHEN YOU PRAY

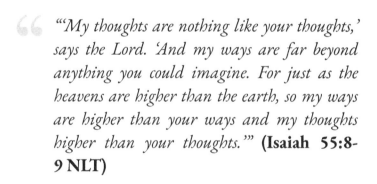 *"'My thoughts are nothing like your thoughts,' says the Lord. 'And my ways are far beyond anything you could imagine. For just as the heavens are higher than the earth, so my ways are higher than your ways and my thoughts higher than your thoughts.'"* **(Isaiah 55:8-9 NLT)**

WHEN WE PRAY, we approach the Maker of the universe, who thought about the creation of the universe, spoke it, and it was there! He operates at a much higher level of power and efficiency than we can even begin to grasp with our finite minds!

Therefore, when we come before Him, we must recalibrate our expectations to a much higher level. We must reach beyond our *"normal"* to access His infinite capabilities.

We honor God when we ask Him for miraculous provisions and interventions. We dishonor Him when we limit Him by acting like He cannot take care of us.

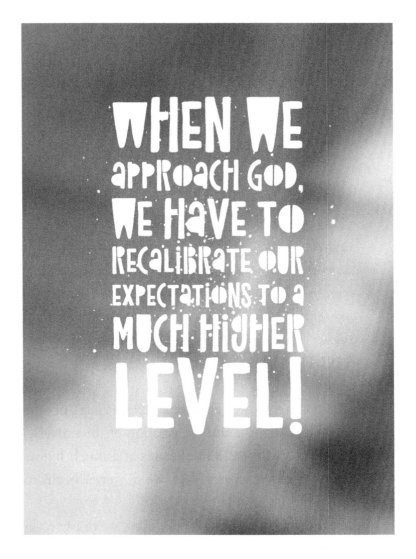

WHEN WE APPROACH GOD, WE HAVE TO RECALIBRATE OUR EXPECTATIONS TO A MUCH HIGHER LEVEL!

Most of us will agree that God can help us *generally*, but we often doubt His willingness to help us *specifically*.

We fuss and worry, constantly thinking that others must be more deserving of His provision than us. As a result, we don't ask and don't receive from His infinite resourcefulness what we desperately need.

We must elevate our thinking to remind ourselves that God can change any situation with a whisper. His words never fall to the ground, powerless and limp:

> *"The rain and snow come down from the heavens and stay on the ground to water the earth. They cause the grain to grow, producing seed for the farmer and bread for the hungry. It is the same with my word. I send it out, and it always produces fruit. It will accomplish all I want it to, and it will prosper everywhere I send it."* **(Isaiah 55:10-11 NLT)**

Do you comprehend just how powerful God is? One word from God creates brand new realities and abundant resources! All He requires of us is to acknowledge His omnipotence. We must approach His throne with the confident knowledge that nothing is impossible for Him:

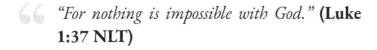

> *"For nothing is impossible with God."* **(Luke 1:37 NLT)**

We must all think much higher when we pray because God is much greater than we can imagine!

STUDY GUIDE:

1. Can you remember times when you were so overwhelmed by the perceived immensity of your problems that you almost felt bad about asking God for His help?
2. Commit to never again talking about your *"mountains of problems"* as if they are challenging for God. God looks down on mountains, not up! Get His perspective on things.
3. Choose to always elevate your thinking to the realm where nothing is impossible for God!
4. Honor God by inviting Him into your challenges. Invite Him to speak a word that will change everything for the better!

REVIEW:

1. Prayer Is Simply Talking And Listening To God.
2. Prayer Should Flow From A Humble Heart.
3. Your Prayers Should Be Confident.
4. Your Prayers Should Be Concise And To The Point.
5. Your Prayers Should Be Consistent And Constant.
6. Pray In Jesus' Name.

7. Pray About Everything!
8. You Do Not Have Because You Don't Ask God.
9. Asking God With The Wrong Motive Doesn't Work.
10. Ask Expecting To Receive From God.
11. Ask God To Bless Your Enemies As You Pray.
12. Ask The Lord To Make You More Loving As You Pray.
13. Make Talking To God A Priority Every Day.
14. Pray According To God's Will.
15. Prayer Frames Help Shape Our Prayers.
16. Ask God To Change The Way You Think.
17. Think At A Higher Level When You Pray.

DAY 18
WHERE THE MIND GOES THE PERSON FOLLOWS

"For as he thinks within himself, so he is." **(Proverbs 23:7 NASB)**

"For as he thinks in his heart, so is he." **(Proverbs 23:7 NKJV)**

THE BIBLE IS evident in its teaching: A person's thinking determines their reality. By implication, if you can change your thinking, you can change your life!

We discussed the importance of thinking at a higher level when talking to God. We continue today by reinforcing that your thoughts determine your life.

If you want to change your life, you must change your thinking. Most of us end up talking to others about what we think most. What we talk about will ultimately shape our actions, attitudes, and outcomes. Please understand that intentional thinking creates intended results.

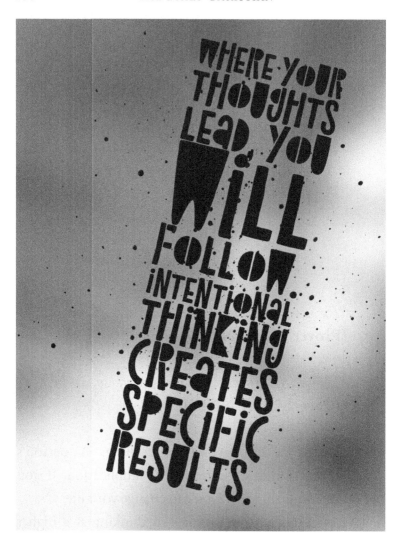

Consider this moment: Your current situation results from yesterday's thoughts. Your current thoughts will influence tomorrow's results. If you are currently thinking a bunch of negative or angry thoughts, there is a good chance it will spill over into negative words, attitudes, and results! Where your thoughts lead, you will follow. It is critical to take responsibility for your thoughts. Nobody else can be assigned to do your thinking!

You and only you can work on this area of your life. Your thinking cannot be delegated to an associate or family member.

If you are negative, praying and asking God for a miracle will be hard. If you cannot ask for that miracle, your situation will remain as negative as your thinking. As a result, you will be... right where your negative thinking led you!

You may wonder how long and often you will have to work to elevate your thinking. I believe you and I will have to work at it as long as we live in this hostile world. No one is exempted. Yet, instead of being overwhelmed by the prospect of life-long vigilance regarding your thinking, be at peace. God is present to help you in your quest! Commit to God and lean on Him to help you. Trust Him to carry you through your battles for positive thoughts:

> *"You will guard him and keep him in perfect and constant peace <u>whose mind</u> both its inclination and its character <u>is stayed on You,</u> because he commits himself to You, leans on You, and hopes confidently in You."* **(Isaiah 26:3 AMP)***(Emphases mine)*

Where is your mind leading you? You can choose!

STUDY GUIDE:

1. If you continue your current train of thought, where will you end up?
2. Make a conscious decision that you will become positive by agreeing with God's opinion of you and what He promised you in the Bible.
3. How can you adjust your thoughts to make room for God's miraculous intervention in your life?
4. Start praying with higher expectations.
5. Start living with greater gratitude.
6. Start believing that you will receive everything you ask of the Lord!

REVIEW:

1. Prayer Is Simply Talking And Listening To God.
2. Prayer Should Flow From A Humble Heart.
3. Your Prayers Should Be Confident.
4. Your Prayers Should Be Concise And To The Point.
5. Your Prayers Should Be Consistent And Constant.

6. Pray In Jesus' Name.
7. Pray About Everything!
8. You Do Not Have Because You Don't Ask God.
9. Asking God With The Wrong Motive Doesn't Work.
10. Ask Expecting To Receive From God.
11. Ask God To Bless Your Enemies As You Pray.
12. Ask The Lord To Make You More Loving As You Pray.
13. Make Talking To God A Priority Every Day.
14. Pray According To God's Will.
15. Prayer Frames Help Shape Our Prayers.
16. Ask God To Change The Way You Think.
17. Think At A Higher Level When You Pray.
18. Where The Mind Goes The Person Follows.

DAY 19
ALWAYS PRAY AND NEVER GIVE UP

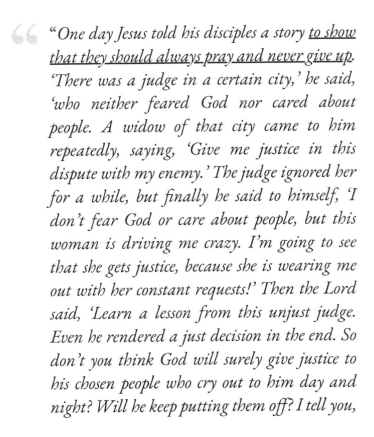

"*One day Jesus told his disciples a story <u>to show
that they should always pray and never give up</u>.
'There was a judge in a certain city,' he said,
'who neither feared God nor cared about
people. A widow of that city came to him
repeatedly, saying, 'Give me justice in this
dispute with my enemy.' The judge ignored her
for a while, but finally he said to himself, 'I
don't fear God or care about people, but this
woman is driving me crazy. I'm going to see
that she gets justice, because she is wearing me
out with her constant requests!' Then the Lord
said, 'Learn a lesson from this unjust judge.
Even he rendered a just decision in the end. So
don't you think God will surely give justice to
his chosen people who cry out to him day and
night? Will he keep putting them off? I tell you,*

he will grant justice to them quickly! But when the Son of Man returns, how many will he find on the earth who have faith?" **(Luke 18:1-8 NLT)***(Emphasis mine)*

THIS STORY REMINDS us that perseverance in prayer will pay off because it takes faith to persevere! God is not only attentive to the prayers of His people; He desires to give them the justice they deserve.

There are a lot of evil dealings in our world, and often God is the only refuge we can find as we suffer from injustice. However, when we allow the thinking of this world to invade our lives, it is easy to give up and stop believing in God. We must remind ourselves that God rewards faith and that faith is often best revealed when the answer seems to be slow in coming.

> *"And it is impossible to please God without faith. Anyone who wants to come to him must believe that God exists and that he rewards those who sincerely seek him."* **(Hebrews 11:6 NLT)***(Emphasis mine)*

As you read the Bible, you will see that many biblical heroes had to persevere through long seasons of waiting for their prayers to be answered.

> *"We do not want you to become lazy, but to imitate those who through faith and patience*

inherit what has been promised.” **(Hebrews 6:12 NIV)***(Emphasis mine)*

Prayers are answered when we persevere through seasons of patient waiting. The widow obtained her answer from an unrighteous judge, and we will similarly get our answers from the *Righteous Judge.*

We must always pray, which takes faith, and we must never give up, which takes patience. This is how we receive what has been promised through prayer and perseverance!

Always pray and never give up!

STUDY GUIDE:

1. Have you given up on some of your prayer requests lately?
2. Have you persevered in your prayers, or did you quit too soon?
3. Remember always to pray (faith) and never to give up (patience and perseverance).

REVIEW:

1. Prayer Is Simply Talking And Listening To God.
2. Prayer Should Flow From A Humble Heart.
3. Your Prayers Should Be Confident.
4. Your Prayers Should Be Concise And To The Point.
5. Your Prayers Should Be Consistent And Constant.
6. Pray In Jesus' Name.
7. Pray About Everything!
8. You Do Not Have Because You Don't Ask God.

9. Asking God With The Wrong Motive Doesn't Work.
10. Ask Expecting To Receive From God.
11. Ask God To Bless Your Enemies As You Pray.
12. Ask The Lord To Make You More Loving As You Pray.
13. Make Talking To God A Priority Every Day.
14. Pray According To God's Will.
15. Prayer Frames Help Shape Our Prayers.
16. Ask God To Change The Way You Think.
17. Think At A Higher Level When You Pray.
18. Where The Mind Goes The Person Follows.
19. Always Pray And Never Give Up.

Day 20
Ask God To Show You What You Need To See

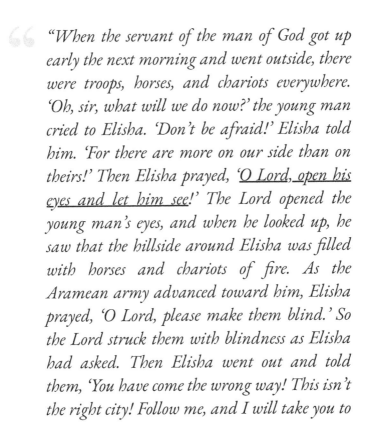

"When the servant of the man of God got up early the next morning and went outside, there were troops, horses, and chariots everywhere. 'Oh, sir, what will we do now?' the young man cried to Elisha. 'Don't be afraid!' Elisha told him. 'For there are more on our side than on theirs!' Then Elisha prayed, 'O Lord, open his eyes and let him see!' The Lord opened the young man's eyes, and when he looked up, he saw that the hillside around Elisha was filled with horses and chariots of fire. As the Aramean army advanced toward him, Elisha prayed, 'O Lord, please make them blind.' So the Lord struck them with blindness as Elisha had asked. Then Elisha went out and told them, 'You have come the wrong way! This isn't the right city! Follow me, and I will take you to *the man you are looking for.' And he led them to the city of Samaria."* **(2 Kings 6:15-19 NLT)***(Emphasis mine)*

HOW OFTEN WE feel like we are under attack, surrounded and utterly defeated by what we see with our natural eyes? This ancient story reminds us that there is a spiritual world with spiritual realities unseen to the human eye.

> *"You, dear children, are from God and have overcome them, because the one who is in you is greater than the one who is in the world."* **(1 John 4:4 NIV)**

It is from that spiritual dimension that our salvation and provision will come when we call upon the Lord in prayer! We need to see that no matter how bad our situation gets, God is always able to rescue us and restore us totally!

We need to see that there are more on our side than on theirs (those who oppose us in this world). Prayer can unlock our spiritual discernment and natural senses to become aware of God's work on our behalf.

Prayer can likewise be used to lock up the senses of our enemies in this world, blinding them and giving us victory!

> *"What shall we say about such wonderful things as these? If God is for us, who can ever be against us?"* **(Romans 8:31 NLT)**

Remind yourself not to be moved by what you see in the natural world around you. Ask God to show you and remind you *"there are more on our side than on theirs."* Ask God to show you what you need to see.

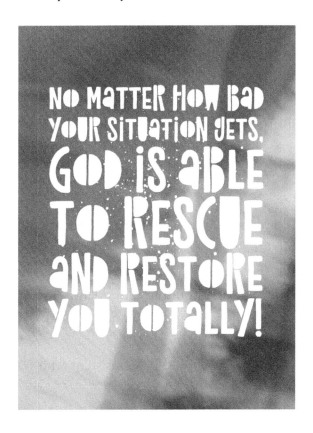

STUDY GUIDE:

1. Have you felt like you are surrounded by calamity on every side? Are you feeling like the enemy is gaining on you and you have no hope?
2. Ask God to show you in the Word how He surrounds you with angels and His love.
3. Now pray like you are part of a victorious majority whose enemy is being led into an ambush of defeat!
4. Take a moment to thank God for His amazing provision and protection.

REVIEW:

1. Prayer Is Simply Talking And Listening To God.
2. Prayer Should Flow From A Humble Heart.
3. Your Prayers Should Be Confident.
4. Your Prayers Should Be Concise And To The Point.
5. Your Prayers Should Be Consistent And Constant.
6. Pray In Jesus' Name.
7. Pray About Everything!
8. You Do Not Have Because You Don't Ask God.

9. Asking God With The Wrong Motive Doesn't Work.

10. Ask Expecting To Receive From God.

11. Ask God To Bless Your Enemies As You Pray.

12. Ask The Lord To Make You More Loving As You Pray.

13. Make Talking To God A Priority Every Day.

14. Pray According To God's Will.

15. Prayer Frames Help Shape Our Prayers.

16. Ask God To Change The Way You Think.

17. Think At A Higher Level When You Pray.

18. Where The Mind Goes The Person Follows.

19. Always Pray And Never Give Up.

20. Ask God To Show You What You Need To See.

Day 21
Lean Into God's Strength With Your Weaknesses

" *"There is therefore now no condemnation to those who are in Christ Jesus, <u>who do not walk according to the flesh</u>, but according to the Spirit."* **(Romans 8:1 NKJV)***(Emphasis mine)*

ONE OF THE biggest challenges of being a believer is that we are still living in a fallen world. Our own weaknesses and shortcomings are very evident as we come into God's perfect Presence to worship and pray. However, we must remember that the Holy Spirit is right there to help us in our moments of weakness!

It is easy to give in to the temptation to buckle under the weight of the condemnation we feel from the enemy. Remember, he is known as *the accuser of the brethren.* There will always be strong opposition to our mission of coming to God with our prayers on a regular basis.

We will do well to remember the words of the apostle Paul to the Corinthian believers:

> *"Each time he said, 'My grace is all you need. My power works best in weakness.' So now I am glad to boast about my weaknesses, so that the*

power of Christ can work through me. That's
why I take pleasure in my weaknesses, and in
the insults, hardships, persecutions, and trou-
bles that I suffer for Christ. <u>For when I am</u>
<u>weak, then I am strong.</u>" (**2 Corinthians**
12:9-10 NLT)*(Emphasis mine)*

We have come to the end of our twenty-one days of
prayer. My prayer is that you will gain strength from the
fact that when you are weak, feeling overwhelmed by trials
and tribulations, and limping from the searing condemnation of your enemy, you can come into God's Presence.

You can rest assured of His acceptance, power, and
grace as you reach out to Him in prayer. He will not turn
away from you, but He will embrace you with His love:

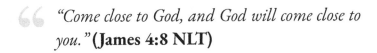 *"Come close to God, and God will come close to*
you." (**James 4:8 NLT**)

Remember this: You can lean into God's strength
with all your weaknesses! Now that you have received
these simple prayer principles, please continue to live by
these principles going forward.

Remember, you are a simple prayer away from God's
reassuring presence! May God bless you with His peace
and His bountiful increase!

STUDY GUIDE:

1. Have you ever felt like you are just too bad of a person to approach God in prayer?
2. Remember that condemnation is a weapon in the hands of our enemy, who will do anything to keep us isolated from God.
3. Have you ever felt weak in your walk for God? Know that that sense of weakness is a great opportunity to approach God for help. A

spring in the desert breaks through the weakest spot in the soil above it. Similarly, God wants to spring up like a fountain through your place of weakness to water your desert moments (See Isaiah 43:19).

4. Take a moment to thank God for your weaknesses and your utter dependence on Him. Then ask Him to work with His power in your weakness!

5. Please don't stop praying. God is ready to receive you wherever and whenever you call upon Him. He will answer you, even when you feel weak and condemned.

REVIEW:

1. Prayer Is Simply Talking And Listening To God.
2. Prayer Should Flow From A Humble Heart.
3. Your Prayers Should Be Confident.
4. Your Prayers Should Be Concise And To The Point.
5. Your Prayers Should Be Consistent And Constant.
6. Pray In Jesus' Name.
7. Pray About Everything!
8. You Do Not Have Because You Don't Ask God.

9. Asking God With The Wrong Motive Doesn't Work.

10. Ask Expecting To Receive From God.

11. Ask God To Bless Your Enemies As You Pray.

12. Ask The Lord To Make You More Loving As You Pray.

13. Make Talking To God A Priority Every Day.

14. Pray According To God's Will.

15. Prayer Frames Help Shape Our Prayers.

16. Ask God To Change The Way You Think.

17. Think At A Higher Level When You Pray.

18. Where The Mind Goes The Person Follows.

19. Always Pray And Never Give Up.

20. Ask God To Show You What You Need To See.

21. Lean Into God's Strength With Your Weaknesses.

ACKNOWLEDGMENTS

Anything worthwhile requires a team of dedicated individuals who are willing to stick to a project until its successful completion. This book is no exception. A big *thank you* to the following individuals who played major roles in the production and completion of the book you hold in your hands!

A big thank you to *the three musketeers* who helped me out with the proofreading and editing of this book: Jill Roberson, Staci Collins, and Debbie Gray. Without your help, I would have been lost and overwhelmed. Thank you for smoothing out the rough edges of my writing, especially when my red and weary eyes couldn't see anymore!

To Melodi and my three boys for your encouragement and willingness to see me disappear into my home office for hours at a time to write this book. You are the lights of my life, and I love you with all my heart!

ABOUT THE AUTHOR

Iann Schonken made the transformative move to the United States from his birthplace, South Africa, in 1988 to pursue theological studies. With great dedication, he earned his Master's Degree in Church Leadership, equipping himself for diverse ministry roles, including administrative duties, public speaking, and consultations.

In 1996, Iann took a significant step by establishing his own non-profit organization, committing himself to his calling across various nations. His mission has taken him to countries such as the United States, Brazil, Mozambique, Madagascar, India, France, the Philippines, Israel, Canada, South Africa, Tanzania, Zambia, and Australia.

Drawing from his extensive ministerial experience spanning over three decades, Iann has notably served as a Lead Pastor in Oceanside, CA, and for 7 years on the executive leadership of Visalia First, a thriving megachurch in Central California. Over the years, he has garnered profound wisdom and knowledge through his diverse roles.

As an accomplished author, Iann has penned several books and created online courses, leaving a lasting impact on his readers and audience. Today, he continues to share his insights as a traveling speaker and author.

Throughout his journey, Iann has been blessed with a fulfilling marriage of over 30 years to his wife, Melodi, and takes immense pride in being a loving father to three children.

For more details about his literary works, artwork, resources, and speaking engagements, visit his website at www.iannschonken.com.

BOOKS BY IANN SCHONKEN

Here are books authored by Iann Schonken. All books available at Amazon.com in various formats:

- *MyPrayerpartner: A Systematic Approach to Prayer (co-authored with his brother, Dr. Johann Schonken).*
- *Simply Supernatural: Believing God For The Impossible Again.*
- *A Person Of His Presence: Welcome God Into Your Busy Life .*
- *Stop Look Listen (To Your Heart).*
- *Remarkable: Extraordinary Life Lessons From The Gospel of Mark.*
- *The Daily Christian: Prayer.*

- *The Daily Christian: Peace.*
- *The Daily Christian: Wisdom.*
- *The Daily Christian: Patience*
- *The Daily Christian: Courage.*

Made in the USA
Middletown, DE
29 October 2023

41489596R00076